CREDIBLE WITNESS
Credible Marriage

by Anetria Pollard

Published by Anetria Pollard Publishing
Copyright © 2023 by Anetria Pollard

ISBN: 979-8-6067-9254-2

All rights reserved. No part of this book may be reproduced in any form or by any electronic or mechanical means, including information storage and retrieval systems, without the permission of the author. Exceptions will be allowed by reviewers for the purpose of quoting brief excerpts.

All scripture, unless otherwise noted is from the KJV of the Bible.

Editorial Contribution and Book Design:
Bridgette Moody-Bridgette Moody Consulting/
www.bridgettemoody.com
bridgette@bridgettemoody.com

Cover Graphics & Design:
Adrienne Brown: distinguishdesingz@gmail.com

Printed in the United States of America

Library of Congress Literary Work
No:1-13320773921

DEDICATION

I dedicate this book to my grandparents Roosevelt and Ophelia Spears. When I was just 13 years old, I marveled at the remarkable milestone of their 50th anniversary. Their enduring love left an indelible mark on me, inspiring a lifelong aspiration to achieve a 50th Golden Wedding Anniversary of my own. Astoundingly, my grandparents surpassed even that, celebrating a remarkable 76 years of marriage.

This dedication is also extended to my neighbors, church, family, friends, Mr. and Mrs. Alfred Pollard II, and countless other couples. I'm indebted to these couples, who, through their unwavering commitment, have shown me the beauty and strength of marriages that endure without succumbing to the challenges life presents.

May this book stand as a testament to the enduring power of love and commitment, echoing the examples set by my grandparents and these remarkable couples, who instilled in me the profound desire to be married until death.

CREDIBLE WITNESS
Credible Marriage

AKNOWLEDGEMENTS

I express my eternal gratitude to God for bestowing upon me the privilege of penning this book, aimed at offering encouragement to fellow couples. It is with heartfelt dedication that I present this work to the countless couples who have weathered the storms of marital challenges, demonstrating unwavering commitment. If anyone comprehends the profound significance of persevering through life's trials, it is undoubtedly you.

My fervent prayer is that your marriage experiences blessings beyond your wildest dreams. I wholeheartedly urge you to never yield, never surrender, and never lose hope. I firmly believe that with unwavering dedication and faithfulness, you have the potential to accomplish anything by putting forth your utmost effort and maintaining unwavering faith.

This project is the result of my relentless faithfulness to God and in believing that I can be successful in my marriage through Christ who strengthens me and guides me.

I extend my heartfelt appreciation to all those who have contributed to this project, whether through their support, insights, or encouragement. Your involvement has been invaluable, and I am profoundly grateful for your contributions. May God's blessings abound in your lives, enriching you in ways beyond measure.

CONTENTS

Introduction: -- 9

Chapter 1: The Most Incredible Witness -- 15

Chapter 2: Embracing Honor -- 21

Chapter 3: The Weight of Accountability -- 33

Chapter 4: Unwavering Persistence --45

Chapter 5: Cultivating Patience -- 57

Chapter 6: The Power of Yielding -- 65

Chapter 7: Finding Happiness Within -- 77

Chapter 8: A Journey of New Beginnings -- 83

About the Author -- 91

CREDIBLE WITNESS
Credible Marriage

INTRODUCTION

In the journey of marriage, an abundant measure of faith is a vital ingredient for success. The union of two souls, sharing life's journey with the one you love, wields incredible power. Anchoring your marital voyage in biblical teachings and harnessing the strength of God's Word to comprehend the fundamental principles of prayer, study, forgiveness, and trust is paramount.

Forgiveness, the cornerstone of enduring love, commences with acknowledging wrongdoing, sincere repentance, turning away from transgressions, accepting forgiveness, and moving forward. The ultimate sacrifice by Jesus has already been made, freeing us from the chains of perpetual pain. Remarkably, God sometimes employs life's most challenging trials to unveil our greatest potential. Personally, each trial I've faced has become a valuable learning opportunity, strengthening my trust in Him. God's faithfulness has never wavered in my life, and I believe He will be equally steadfast in yours. Whatever your heart desires, present it to God in faith, believing that His response will exceed all expectations. He is the source of everything you need.

Periodically, invite God to cleanse your inner self and reveal the marriage He envisioned for you. Like a well-coordinated football team, huddle together with God and your spouse to strategize. Openly discuss your concerns and seek God's guidance in resolving them. Building a united team, committed to doing whatever it takes, is imperative. Teammates collaborate and support each other, working toward a shared objective.

Never hesitate to place your trust in each other. Lean on your partner when you require assistance and be there for them likewise. Address problems by acknowledging their presence and seek resolution, either through mutual efforts or professional assistance if necessary.

Great faith blossoms when profound trust prevails. The Bible serves as your steadfast guide. Remember, external sources cannot fix your marital issues; they may offer temporary solace but lack the power of lasting transformation. As Bishop TD Jakes wisely advises, "Never make a permanent decision based on a temporary situation."

Embrace God's Word as the cornerstone for fortifying your marriage. Grasping the principles of matrimony is the key to a lasting partnership. Marriage, in its essence, is truly remarkable. When God created man and woman, He envisioned the beauty of harmonious unions. *Proverbs 18:22a* reminds us, *"Whoso findeth a wife findeth a good thing,"* emphasizing that marriage is a divine institution, blessed by God Himself.

Sometimes, marriages need an extra spark to rekindle the flame. Exhibit affection and express appreciation through meaningful gestures. Assist with household tasks, share intimate moments, and convey love through affectionate words, praise, and gratitude.

Actions, more than words, gratitude. Actions, more than words, manifest and reciprocate love.

In this pursuit, I, Anetria Pollard, aim to share my witness of 38 years of a thriving and joyful marriage. Your path to happiness may differ, but a significant part of my success emanates from our unwavering faith and trust in God. Marriage stands as a sacred covenant between a man and a woman, where the power of spoken words, in alignment with God's Word, holds incredible influence. Therefore, speak life into your marriage.

Maintain your focus, guarding against the distractions of trivial matters. Your destiny is too precious to grant undue importance to elements beyond the scope of your marriage. Stay attuned to what is true, honorable, right, excellent, praiseworthy, and of good report. If it does not meet these standards, divert your thoughts and attention away from it.

Your marriage merits unwavering dedication: just as Jesus commanded Satan to step aside, you possess the power to do the same. Speak it forth.

When the adversary attempts to overwhelm you, sow the Word of God. We are encouraged to speak with purpose, for God intends for us to be vocal about our faith and desires.

Chapter One
Most Credible Witness

In *Genesis 2:22-23*, we find the beautiful account of God creating woman from man's rib and presenting her to him. Adam joyfully exclaimed, "*This now is bone of my bones and flesh of my flesh; she shall be called Woman, because she was taken out of man.*" This passage marks the inception of the sacred bond of marriage.

From this divine act, God stands as the greatest witness to the institution of marriage. At the very dawn of humanity, God recognized that man should not journey through life alone. Thus, from Adam's rib, He fashioned a "help meet," creating Eve. As they became one, God's design for marriage was unmistakably established, a perfect and precious gift from the Creator.

It is no wonder that *Proverbs 18:22* proclaims, *"Whosoever findeth a wife findeth a good thing and obtaineth favour of the Lord."* God's blueprint for man and woman in the Garden of Eden set the foundation for the marital union. God, in His wisdom, ordained that man should have a partner to share life's journey.

In *Proverbs 31:10-14*, we gain insight into the attributes of a noble wife: one who is more precious than rubies, trusted by her husband, industrious, and resourceful. She exemplifies strength and dignity, her wisdom a source of guidance. This virtuous wife diligently manages her household, earning the blessings and praises of her family. It is a reminder that a woman who reveres the Lord deserves honor above all else.

The sacred verse in *Genesis 2:24* underscores the union of marriage, declaring, *"That is why a man leaves his father and mother and is united to his wife, and they become one flesh."*
It signifies the divine design of marriage, wherein two individuals unite in a bond so profound that they

become one. Marriage is indeed a gift from God, He has bestowed upon us the recipe for its success. Sacrificial love, as demonstrated by husbands in *Ephesians 5:28-33*, mirrors the love of Christ for His church. In God's wisdom, He has equipped us to make marriages credible, loving, and lasting. When God calls us to, He provides the means to achieve. He will not falter. Notably, God serves as our Credible Witness and Credible Marriage counselor, offering His guidance through His Word. We have the choice to accept or reject His wisdom, but God, in His omniscience, knows what is best for us.

The sanctity of marriage is reaffirmed in *Matthew 19:5-6*, where Jesus upholds the sacredness of the marital bond, declaring, *"What therefore God has joined, let not man put asunder."* This divine significance is further accentuated in the second chapter of John, where Jesus blesses a marriage celebration and performs His inaugural miracle, turning water into wine. The divine blueprint for marriage, as illustrated in the Bible, serves as the enduring foundation for credible and lasting unions. God, the ultimate witness, stands ready to guide and support those who seek to build their marriages upon His wisdom and love.

Journal

Chapter Two
EMBRACING HONOR

What is Marriage?

The Concise Bible Dictionary beautifully encapsulates marriage as: "The union of one man and one woman in covenant commitment for a lifetime, second only to their commitment to God." In the sacred bond of marriage, selfishness finds no dwelling. It is a ministry where two souls unite, witnessed by both God and man. Let the radiant love of God illuminate your actions, nurturing the very essence of your relationship.

Countless individuals have observed my husband and me, noting the palpable connection reflected in the way we gaze at each other. They say my eyes light up when I speak of him. Such is the spark that marriage should embody, a testament to the divine presence within your relationship. Always approach each other with sensitivity and a generous heart. Giving in a marriage transcends mere receipt; it is a spiritual commitment and a testament to our faith in one another. Give faithfully, and witness the abundant blessings that God bestows upon your lives. You might very well be the instrument through which God works. Regardless of your life or marital stage, remember the promise, *"Give, and it shall be given unto you; good measure, pressed down, and shaken together, and running over, shall men give into your bosom" (Luke 6:38a).*

Love as you wish to be loved. While reciprocity is not guaranteed, love in marriage mirrors agape, the highest form of love encompassing charity and God's love for humanity. It is unconditional and transformative. To change the dynamics of your relationship, embody the self-sacrificial love you desire. Surrender to God's plan and let Him be the head of your marriage. Remain resolute, and do not compromise by giving in to quitting. See strength and endurance throughout your marriage journey. Always be open to God's ordained purpose, boldly declaring yourselves an anointed couple, deeply favored, rooted in love, unwavering in faith, bold in action, diligently seeking the Lord, and destined to conquer through Jesus Christ. Amen! Having witnessed numerous unhappy unions, I resolved to fight for the credibility of my marriage. I vowed to cultivate a marriage filled with genuine love and joy, one that stands as a testament to the beauty and fulfillment of true love. In the face of challenges, resist the urge to give up. Remember the biblical admonition, *"What therefore God hath joined together, let no man put asunder" (Mark 10:9).*

I stand as a living witness that marriage can serve as a gateway to a deeper, more intimate relationship with both God and your spouse. Embrace trust, for as these relationships flourish, you become more attuned to your emotions, attitudes, needs, and abilities. Through Christ's strength, you can overcome all things. Be an overcomer and remain open to continuous improvement. *"Wherefore seeing we also are compassed about with so great a cloud of witnesses, let us lay aside every weight, and the sin which doth so easily beset us and let us run with patience the race that is set before us" (Hebrews 12:1).*

As Rick Warren wisely puts it, "If you really love someone, then you show it by how you act toward that person." Love transcends mere attraction or sentimentality; it is a powerful and unwavering force. People walk together for shared goals and values that strengthen relationships. In marriage, two individuals walk united for a common purpose: LOVE. Let love be your guiding force, for, as the scripture says, *"Wherefore they are no more twain, but one flesh. What therefore God hath joined, let not man put asunder" (Matthew 19:6).*

Our Marriage Story

My husband was fortunate to grow up in a household where both parents provided unwavering support and nurturing. On the other hand, my upbringing was under the dynamic care of a single mother, a powerhouse who worked tirelessly to provide for her three children. Despite the differences, we never lacked anything.

My husband got along well with his parents and I with my mother. Our parents played instrumental roles in our life, taking us to church, participating in school activities, and ensuring our well-being. Ironically, we both battled with asthma growing up and we both experienced similar surgeries.

Fate wove our paths together at Southern University in Baton Rouge, Louisiana, back in 1983. Graduating in 1984 with BA Degrees in Liberal Arts-Mass Communication, our journey from acquaintances to an inseparable couple began in the spring of 1983. Introducing him to my mother during spring break revealed he was the first guy she genuinely liked. The feeling was mutual when he took me to meet his family in Michigan that summer. His parent's warm welcome marked the commencement of our union.

Our personalities are robust, once a no-nonsense couple that has mellowed with age. Quick decisions now come effortlessly, liberated from concerns about external opinions. Fun-loving is our mantra—a love that endures and inspires others.

Our passion resonates authentically, emphasizing the importance of excellence in marriage.

We've attained "Silver, Pearl and Coral" levels in our marriage. While far from perfect, our union serves as a vessel for God's glory. Like the perfectly round pearl, our marriage is unique and valuable. Comparisons are futile; instead, fashion your marriage after how Christ loved the church. Silver symbolizes value, marking our 25th anniversary as an epiphany of God's goodness in bringing two diverse individuals together. Coral represents happiness and value, a stage we embrace with joy and mutual appreciation. Each level—silver, pearl, coral—reflects God's strengthening and preservation of our marriage, a testimony to His glory on earth. Living in different states away from family, we've relied on each other and God.

Unintimidated, our marriage stands firm, anchored by God at its core. Expressions of love, be it a kiss, smile, encouragement, respect, or honest communication, define our daily routine. Mutual love and affection form the bedrock of our successful marriage. As the psalm reminds us, "Be still and know that I am God: I will be exalted among the heathen; I will be exalted in the earth" (Psalms 46:10).

Our two children, born in July 1985 and September 1987, enriched our union. Our journey has been remarkably problem-free, grounded in the understanding that we are one, steadfastly there for each other. The lyrics of "I got you, Babe" encapsulate our commitment—we have each other and God.

Our marriage is the cornerstone of our family, ordained by God, and we seek His blessing daily. Honesty, listening, and being each other's confidant have fortified our relationship. My husband is my best friend, and our commitment spans heart, mind, body, and soul. As a result, we have never been separated, nor have we ever discussed it. Divorce is not an option. Throughout our marriage we have sought to love God and accept each other despite our imperfections. When my husband found me, he found a soulmate. We complete each other in our platonic relationship. The bible tells us, "He who findeth a wife finds a good thing" (Proverbs 18:22a). In the realm of good marriages, we acknowledge that relationships are a paramount commitment, demanding our best efforts. From a young age, I aspired to a successful marriage and remain committed to making it a reality. As Nelson Mandela wisely said, "I never lose. I either win or learn."

Today is an opportunity to transform your relationship, to work for it, and recognize your royalty within it. Our roles as spiritual leaders have strengthened our marriage, fostering accountability and leadership. Our divine connection, a result of being in the right place at the right time, inspires us to remain focused for life. We understand that by staying in the will of God, He will bless us and our marriage, and every day, in every way, we want Jesus in our marriage.

A Prayer for Marriage

"Heavenly Father, I offer profound gratitude for the sacred bond of marriage that you have graciously overseen from its inception. My wife and I thank you for the ebb and flow of life, your mercy and grace have been our steadfast companions, holding us firmly through both the joys and challenges, a testament to your righteous hand.

In embracing the role of a servant for Jesus Christ, I've discovered the profound lessons that make me a better husband and father. I am indebted, Lord, for the wealth of knowledge and divine wisdom you provide to navigate, console, and nurture our marriage. Your continuous investment in our spirits, entwined with yours, echoes the truth that a cord of three strands is unbreakable, as your word declares.

Extend your healing touch, I implore, over marriages currently weathering storms. I rebuke the forces of darkness and call upon Jehovah Nissi, for in you, Lord, victory reigns. Silence every dissenting tongue and let the Prince of Peace shower love upon these unions, empowering them with words of wisdom, inspiration, and guidance. May the fruit of our lips resound in glory for your wondrous works.

Dear Lord, I entreat your Divine grace to be our refuge in times of need throughout the journey of unity. This prayer is offered in the name of Jesus. Amen!" (Rod Pollard)

Journal

Chapter Three
THE WEIGHT OF ACCOUNTABILITY

June 1, 1985, stands etched in the tapestry of my life as one of the most joyous days. On that radiant day, I joyfully uttered the words "I Do" to the love of my life. Every detail of our wedding was a kaleidoscope of colors, mirroring God's promise of peace and serenity in a beautiful rainbow-themed ceremony. My wish upon a rainbow was granted, and for 38 years, I have been the cherished bride to my handsome, sexy, and God-fearing husband.

Our wedding, a stunning affair on a scorching summer Saturday afternoon, was a tapestry of love, music, family, and friends. The unity candle symbolically joined our families for a lifetime, a moment more beautiful than my wildest dreams.

Bridesmaids adorned in hues of baby blue, lime green, orange, yellow, peach, midnight blue, salmon, fuchsia, and purple added a vibrant touch.

In my ivory gown, with a lace bodice adorned with hand-laid pearls over a satin skirt, I was the epitome of bridal grace. If my husband were to ask for my hand again, my response would resound with the same unwavering "Yes!" Prior to our nuptials, we sought marriage counseling from my pastor, who equipped us with the essential tools for healthy communication. We pondered the question of why we were getting married, and our resolute answer, "We loved each other and wanted to spend the rest of our lives together," set the foundation. We understood the gravity of marriage, a commitment lasting until death do us part.

Our wedding song, "Endless Love," resonated with our enduring commitment. True agape love defines us, a love meant to be an inspiration to ourselves and others. Our journey has been marked by a resolute determination to live out the vows we took before the Lord.

Intimidation has never swayed us, for no one has the right to jeopardize our commitment. We have a divine design, perfectly tailored for each other. The Lord orchestrated our union, and our sensitivity to this commitment for life keeps us accountable. Having witnessed the enduring love of my grandparents, married for **76 years** until God called my granddad home, I aspired to emulate their commitment. Our marriage has been a testament to God's remarkable work, growing and holding each other accountable.

Our faithfulness has not gone unnoticed, and God's favor is evident in our union. Asking and receiving, I prayed for a good husband, and I am blessed with one who loves and adores me. Marriage, we believe, is a promising job if you give it your all, resist temptation, and work towards intimacy, happiness, companionship, trust, and passion.

Every day is a new opportunity to rectify past mistakes and embrace the lessons of yesterday as steppingstones to a better tomorrow. Problems, we recognize, come to make us strong. According to my husband, marriage is the union of two joined together to navigate life's journey, support each other through ups and downs and remain committed.

Relying on God's strength taps into something real and lasting. "Do not be dismayed, for I am your God. I will strengthen you and help you; I will uphold you with my righteous right hand" (**Isaiah 41:10 NIV**). A Christ-based marriage draws strength from God, our shield. Pouring out His power in our relationship, we find all we need in His word. Life may not always appear ideal, but during such times, we turn to the Bible, taking heart in Jesus' promise never to leave or forsake us. Even in less-than-perfect circumstances, as Christians, we trust in Him. Growth, we've learned, comes through commitment to love.

Marriage, to us, is a bond where two people share their uniqueness. Disagreements are met with mutual understanding and respect for each other's thoughts. Constantly striving for opportunities to grow, we remind ourselves of the beauty and specialness of our relationship, reinforcing our commitment. Seeking forgiveness is part of our journey. "But if you do not forgive others their sins, your Father will not forgive your sins" (**Matthew 6:15 NIV**).

Ephesians 4:31-32 guides us, urging us to put away bitterness, anger, and malice, and instead be kind, tenderhearted, and forgiving. Ephesians 6:10 echoes the call to be strong in the Lord and the power of His might. "And we know that all things work together for good to them that love God, to them who are the called according to His purpose" (Romans 8:28).

The Witness of Trials

My marital journey, though far from flawless, has been a tapestry woven with remarkable experiences. Each challenge, no matter how arduous, has become a steppingstone for me to elevate my praise for God. I've emerged as a steadfast witness to His magnificence within the intricate dynamics of my marriage. It's a testament that nothing is beyond God's ability.

Acknowledging the hurdles, I've faced; I recognize they've been instrumental in sculpting me into a credible witness for others. My life unfolds like a song, a melody composed to reveal that no obstacle exists that God cannot guide me through. Trials are an inherent facet of life, a shared reality that binds us together. I'm not alone; God has orchestrated my steps to be a blessing not only to my generation but to those that follow. In gratitude, I lift my voice, thanking the Lord for blessing my marriage. What the adversary intended for harm, God, in His infinite wisdom, has turned to my advantage. I've traversed too great a distance to surrender now. Faith is not a passive stance; it requires active engagement. We work for a cause greater than ourselves, a lifetime investment. *Psalm 91:9-10* resonates in my heart, providing solace: *"Because thou hast made the Lord, which is my refuge, even the Most-High, thy habitation; There shall no evil befall thee, neither shall any plague come nigh thy dwelling."* In the realm of elevated praise, we discover a sanctuary, a higher place of worship that bestows rest. God beckons us to this elevated plane, a realm of praise that transcends our storms. In moments of turmoil, I draw strength from Him, realizing that He has equipped me with everything I need.

As Dr. Michelle Bengtson wisely notes, forgiveness is not about forgetting but entrusting the situation to God's capable hands. Trials serve to fortify us; God stands beside us, ready to rectify what is amiss. Faith becomes the impetus to persevere until His righteous resolution unfolds. The assurance echoes: "No weapon formed against us shall prosper." God stands unwavering, fulfilling His promises. Together, my spouse and I weathered physical ailments, yet our commitment endured. In sickness and health, we nursed each other back to wholeness. These experiences transformed me into a living testimony of God's healing power. My praise becomes a confounding force against the enemy.

Embracing the certainty that God desires the best for us, I hold onto the belief that His promises are true. Covered by the enduring power of Jesus' blood, I face each trial with unwavering confidence. His unchanging nature anchors me in the storm, and I find joy in being a beacon for other marriages. Building on a foundation of profound friendship, I work towards a stronger relationship. I echo the biblical wisdom of speaking into existence that which is not. Trusting and worshipping God in spirit and truth opens the floodgates of His favor. In my weakness, He is the great "I Am." True accountability surfaces when God takes precedence in every aspect of life, and strength is found in acknowledging one's spouse as a divine gift. God's reminders of past victories serve as beacons of hope for future challenges.

God's multifaceted nature as a healer, provider, and deliverer assures that every need in marriage is met. Singing a new song to the Lord, I seek an increased capacity to receive His blessings. Recognizing the blessing within the storm, I'm thankful for the preparation that equips me to help others through writing. Maya Angelou's words resonate: "Having courage does not mean that we are unafraid. Having courage and showing courage means we face our fears. We are able to say, I have fallen, but I will get up." "Trust in the Lord with all thine heart and lean not unto thine own understanding. In all thy ways acknowledge him, and He shall direct thy path" (Proverbs 3:5-6). Trusting in the Lord with all my heart, I acknowledge that my source and supply is in God. His provisions sustain my marriage. Reflecting on the past, my husband and I overflow with gratitude for God's abundant blessings. His grace and mercy have shielded us from adversities. Today, we choose blessings, confident that the will of God prevails. Encouragement abounds—learn from experiences, be resilient in difficulty and stay committed.

Terri L. Orbach aptly notes, "Long lasting, happy marriages have more than great communication. Instead, you must be nice to your partner." Small, consistent gestures matter. Resolving issues and committing to staying together fortifies the foundation of an enduring union.

Journal

Chapter Four
UNWAVERING PERSISTENCE

I aspire to share words that uplift and enrich your marital journey. May you be endowed with the strength to live abundantly in faith, becoming a source of positive influence for other marriages. Surrender to God's will and let His transformative power shape both you and your union. In the realm of divine ordinances, everything aligns with God's righteousness; it's a stark contrast to the fallibility of human nature. The omnipotence of God can effectuate profound change in you and your marriage, and when He declares a thing, no mortal voice can say no.

Couples often harbor realistic expectations about the complexities of marriage and relationships.

With time, cohabitation unveils deeper layers of understanding and acceptance for your partner. Perseverance, a key ingredient, intertwines with affection. It is paramount never to succumb to the temptation of surrender. Instead, persistently strive to fortify your marriage, where attentive listening becomes as crucial as expressing your thoughts.

Persistent efforts act as a shield, fending off unnecessary problems that seek to sow discord. Transform problems into steppingstones and maintain unwavering faith, even in the face of apparent desolation. Empowerment lies in embracing the Word and translating it into action, loving wholeheartedly while seeking wisdom from those with more experience.

Submitting to God in genuine worship becomes a potent tool. Disturb God a little, as illustrated in Luke 18:5a, where persistence yields divine response. It says, "Yet because this widow troubled me, I will avenge her…" Amidst life's storms, find solace in God's protective embrace, tapping into His omnipotence for victory. If your marriage feels joyless, seek ways to infuse happiness while awaiting transformation. Persevere, for your marriage is invaluable; keep the flame alive in your eyes. Embrace the incredible wealth of being a child of the Most-High God, manifesting affection through gestures that convey genuine appreciation. Fighting for your marriage entails a spiritual retreat—enter your closet, delve into the Scriptures, and pray fervently. Bother God, for He welcomes your entreaties. Cultivate expectancy and let the prayer of faith salvage your marriage. Invite the anointing and power of God to cleanse and transform.

Express unwavering support and belief in your partner, conveying love through various means. Rediscover accountability and persistence as indispensable elements to sustain marital happiness. Abide by God's directives, and He will stand by you. Uphold His Word, for it works when you work it. Communication, a vital artery in marriage, requires a reciprocal flow. Pause amidst self-absorption to listen earnestly to your partner.

Embrace your flaws, recognizing their role in personal growth. Transform from within and ask God to unleash the mighty power within you. Appreciate and celebrate each other, accepting God's plan for your marriage. Blessings will cascade like rain in spring when you align with His purpose. Give thanks in all things, and let gratitude permeate your union. With God's guidance, a joyful marriage is within reach.

Pastor James Ford emphasizes the protective roles of spouses and underscores love as an action verb exercised in various dimensions of the relationship. He advocates for a spiritual cleansing, akin to a sorbet, using the Word of God to purify hearts from past hurts and detrimental influences.

Continue to Date

If you follow me on social media, you have probably noticed that my husband and I date. Our date night is usually on Friday. Typically, it is pre-planned time we have carved out to spend some quality time together after a busy work week. We do different things as we get away to spend quality time with each other. Date night shows that we are a couple. We usually go out to dinner, to movies, etc. Anything that allows us to focus on us completely. We love trying new places and food. At least twice a year we really do it up. He does not mind doing it for me. We deserve it, he says. Our policy is to come together and re-energize each other.

Dating gives life to a relationship. We all remember those amazing date nights when he was trying to impress you. They are still important. There is a difference between going to dinner and going on a date. Dating is romantic. My husband promised me he would continue doing the things he did when he met me.

One that is most meaningful to me is whenever we are together, and we then go in different directions he always kisses me before we walk away and when we reunite. Date night is one of my favorite times of the week. I love getting ready for him, looking pretty and fresh. We reminisce and unwind by focusing on us. The phones are off limits, and we seldom double date. We occasionally share meals. It is so romantic. Take the limits off your marriage and do something different. Date again, love again, respect again, travel again, and put God first again. After thirty-eight years of marriage, I am still learning to appreciate our differences and most importantly how much we have grown to be so much alike. Do not let your current condition control how you do things for the rest of your life. Get back to dating and courting each other again.

It is worth the expense, yet it does not have to be expensive. It is not the cost of the date, but it is the quality time you spend together. Dating and vacationing takes the relationship to the next level. "You can't change the next chapter in your life if you keep re-reading the last one" (Unknown). "Healing is not a doctrine. It's straight out of the Heart of God because He loves you and me" (Gloria Copeland). Let your marriage be a gift to others that demonstrates how to honor each other. Arise! Shine! We get one shot at life, so make a difference by having a successful marriage. God created you for purpose. Your marriage has the purpose to strengthen someone else's marriage.

Remember, the Lord answers prayer according to His will. I believe anyone God has joined has the propensity to behave a certain way when they get married or planning to get married. Birds have the propensity to fly, and couples have the propensity to grow together. Seek God first in your marriage. "True love stands by each other's side on good days and stands closer on bad days" (Unknown). I cannot overemphasize this importance. Does your marriage have a kingdom agenda? Have you placed your marriage under God's authority? I deeply encourage you to do so.

If we do not seek first the Kingdom of God, nothing will be added. Don't you want all the blessings God can add to your marriage? They are beyond what you can even think or imagine. Victory belongs to Jesus and to you if you obey God's Word.

Putting my spouse first is paramount. It is a witness of respect when you are polite and kind. Your marriage is a witness to what God has joined and what He is doing in this union. ***Ephesians 5:33*** *says, "However, each one of you also must love his wife as he loves himself, and the wife must respect her husband" (NIV).* Your marriage is a witness of the power of unity by God. You have been joined. Let everyone see why you are in love. No matter what you face, God will bring you through. It is for all the world to see that you have purpose and destiny. Jesus prayed in John 17 asking the Father to keep those who have believed and will believe unified against the world and the devil.

Marriage Prayer

Heavenly Father, I express gratitude for the institution of marriages. Lord, I implore your healing touch on wounded hearts and seek your guidance for those in search of answers. May a fresh wind of your spirit breathe life into their unions. Inspire husbands and wives who are grappling with financial challenges, offering them innovative money management solutions and the wisdom to enhance their financial situations with multiple streams of income.

May your hedge of protection surround their families, and may you instill in them the resilience to cling to their faith. Father, I acknowledge the blessing of a remarkable spouse who loves me unconditionally. Strengthen the core of our relationship and extend your blessings to those reading this prayer. May the words spoken here serve as a source of practical guidance to enhance their marriages and deepen their commitment. Guide couples to discover common ground upon which they can stand firm. Instill forgiveness and joy anew in marriages, declaring victory even as we patiently await your transformative work, understanding that scars can serve as reminders of your redemptive power.

Father, I thank you for your continuous hand in marriages, orchestrating the resolution of challenges. Provide for those in need and help us recognize that challenges come to fortify our strength. I express gratitude for leading me from a place of despair into the illuminating light of your son, Jesus Christ. I give glory for your ongoing work, standing firm on the assurance found in Proverbs 19:23, which declares, "The fear of the Lord tendeth to life: and he that hath it shall abide satisfied; he shall not be visited with evil."

Father, grant us the understanding of your Word so that we may experience victory, irrespective of our pasts. May peace and joy flood our lives, ushering in healthy and triumphant marriages for each one of us. Thank you, Lord, for allowing us to encounter your strength and finding satisfaction in your abundant blessings. In the name of Jesus, I pray. Amen.

Journal

Chapter Five
CULTIVATING PATIENCE

"Love is patient, love is kind. It does not envy, it does not boast, it is not proud. It does not dishonor others; it is not self-seeking. It is not easily angered; it keeps no record of wrongs. Love does not delight in evil but rejoices with the truth. It always protects, always trusts, always hopes, always perseveres" (1 Corinthians 13:4-7 NIV).

The Power of Love:

"This selfless love, a prelude to marriage, demands a thorough inspection of strongholds—those insidious distractions that assail our thoughts. Our journey led us to the sanctuary of marriage counseling, an invaluable compass guiding us toward effective communication and a unified focus on "us." Wisdom, a stalwart ally, is indispensable in the face of the enemy's deceptive tactics, weaving lies such as the pursuit of perfection, selfish prioritization, financial segregation, and the haunting echoes of past relationships."

"Understanding that marriage is imbued with purpose immunizes couples against potential pitfalls. It necessitates confronting unresolved issues before the sacred union. Our faith reminds us of an ideal God capable of crafting a sublime marriage, urging us to introspect before taking the plunge into matrimony."
"Marriage, a sacred pact and lifelong commitment, thrives on diligent effort. 'A sacred relationship is one in which the Divine is discerned in the other. Recognizing that we are not just bodies, but vessels of love and truth fuels a profound desire to experience this sacred love in our relationships' (Unknown). Loving someone is only half the equation; addressing the strongholds gripping our minds completes the journey."

"The tendrils of strongholds delve into the depths of our hearts and souls, rooting themselves, and rewiring our thoughts. Yet, remember always: you are defined by what God says, and surrender not your thoughts to the devil, the father of lies. His mission, clear and malevolent, is to kill, steal, and destroy. "Reprogramming our minds, purging them of the devil's negativity, requires steadfast commitment. We must not water the seeds of deceit and must fight for the truth. Embracing the Word of God, speaking it, praying it, and seeking help are pivotal for a robust marital foundation."

"Life begets hope, and trust becomes the linchpin of a thriving marriage. Prioritizing the sanctity of marriage, internalizing the Word of God, and its application are imperative. A flourishing marriage, much like a well-tended garden, requires continuous care."

"Marriage ministry stands as a bulwark, maintaining the wholesomeness of families. Acknowledging the potential for learning and growth through marriage counseling fosters resilience against weaknesses. Understand that challenges are transient; a negative force succumbs to a positive counterforce. Satisfaction and joy emerge from earnest efforts." "At times, seeking professional help becomes imperative. Divine intervention can manifest through counseling, a safe space for honesty and growth. 'The person challenging you and holding you accountable truly loves you, surpassing those who watch you stagnate' (Unknown). Imagine exuding a vibe that compels the enemy to reconsider. Say yes to a successful marriage, resisting the devil's lies with a resounding no."

"Claim your voice, usher in positive, love-inducing change, and trust that God will safeguard you. His grace and mercy, perennial and replenishing, await. If grace is needed, seek it boldly. Stand firm, knowing that God orchestrates your steps. Building muscle may feel peculiar at first, but it's a testament to your commitment." *"Faith, the substance of hopeful things, and the evidence of the unseen, can move mountains" (Hebrews 11:1).* Embrace a positive faith in a positive God, receiving His blessings. Persevere when others falter. Be an overcomer. Believe that you will make it and pray for your marriage's resilience." *"As steadfast Corinthians, be unmovable, always abounding in the work of the Lord, for your labor is not in vain" (1 Corinthians 15:58).* Your dedication is not futile; endure, continue giving, guiding by God's love.

Cling to His unchanging hand and anchor your hope and marriage in eternal truths. Stay committed to the oneness you've vowed to uphold."

Marriage Prayer:

Lord be in our marriage and so abide with us that we may dwell together in harmony and trust. God, be in our marriage and grant us love in surplus that we, loving each other may also love Thy purpose. God be in our marriage and in our dreams and plans that we may build together a Christian home that stands. God be in our marriage as we blend lives together that all may hear our songs: This marriage is forever!

(Terry Tanksley)

Journal

Chapter Six
THE POWER OF YIELDING

"But the wisdom that is from above is first pure, then peaceable, gentle, willing to yield, full of mercy and good fruits, without partiality and without hypocrisy"
(James 3:17 NKJV).

"Yielding, a term rich in meaning, symbolizes the art of gracefully giving way under life's pressures, embracing a gentle flexibility rather than rigid resistance. It's about being inclined to give in, a dance of submission and compliance that transcends mere surrender—it's a mutual embrace of selflessness.

In the realm of marriage, purpose unfolds when we yield not just to each other but also to the divine guidance of God. The tapestry of a meaningful union is woven when spouses yield to the needs, thoughts, and dreams of one another, echoing the biblical examples that advocate for this harmonious give-and-take. Placing God at the forefront, prioritizing His examples, becomes the cornerstone, for, as the scriptures wisely state, 'a house divided cannot stand alone.' It is in the mutual uplifting, where each partner feels like a superhero, that the foundation of an unshakable bond is laid.

Expressing gratitude for the lessons learned, we acknowledge God's role in teaching us to yield to His will in our love affair, fostering an open-minded approach to each other's thoughts and ideas. Yielding becomes a comprehensive commitment— not merely giving in but also securing each other's blessings and embracing the virtue of patience, nurturing a fruit that stands the test of time.

Yielding, in its profound essence, extends beyond the confines of marital dynamics. It beckons us to yield to God through acts of giving, tithes, prayer, the study of His Word, and unwavering obedience, building a sacred covenant rooted in trust and eternal truths. As we tend to God's house with diligence, His benevolence extends to ours—a reciprocal relationship where care begets care.

Resisting the allure of temptation, we yield to the promise of happiness, inspired by hope. The path to a grounded relationship involves an unwavering commitment to togetherness and oneness. Shifting the focus from 'me' to 'we,' we embrace the reality that unity is not merely a merger but a state of harmonious unification, a wholeness composed of two intertwining souls."

Marriage Truths...

The ancient wisdom of the scriptures resonates with timeless truths about marriage:

- *"And the Lord God said, It is not good that man should be alone; I will make him a help meet for him"* ***(Genesis 2:18)***.

- *"Therefore, shall a man leave his father and his mother, and shall cleave unto his wife: and they shall be one flesh"* ***(Genesis 2:24)***.

- *"Whoso findeth a wife findeth a good thing. And obtaineth favour of the Lord"* ***(Proverbs 18:22)***.

❖ *"Take ye wives, and begat sons and daughters; and take wives for your sons, and give your daughters to husbands, that they may bear sons and daughters; that ye may be increased there, and not diminished"* ***(Jeremiah 29:6)***.

❖ *"And I will betroth thee unto me forever; yea, I will betroth thee unto me in righteousness, and in judgement, and in loving kindness, and in mercies. I will even betroth thee unto me in faithfulness; and thou shalt know the Lord"* ***(Hosea 2:19, 20)***.

❖ *"Nevertheless, to avoid fornication, let every man have his own wife, and let every woman have her own husband. Let the husband render unto the wife due benevolence: and likewise, also the wife unto the husband. The wife hath not power of her own body, but the husband: and likewise, also the husband hath not power of his own body, but the wife"* ***(I Corinthians 7:2-4)***.

❖ *"I will therefore that the younger women marry, bear children, guide the house, give no occasion to the adversary to speak reproachfully"* ***(I Timothy 5:14)***.

❖ *"Marriage is honorable in all, and the bed undefiled: but whoremongers and adulterers God will judge"* ***(Hebrews 13:4)***.

❖ *Wives submit yourselves unto your own husbands, as unto the Lord. For the husband is the head of the wife, even as Christ is the head of the church: and he is the savior of the body. Therefore, as the church is subject unto Christ, so let the wives be to their own husbands in everything. Husbands, love your wives even as Christ loved the church, and gave Himself for it; That he might sanctify and cleanse it with the washing of water by the Word. That He might present to Himself a glorious church, not having spot, or wrinkle, or any such thing; but that it should be holy and without blemish. So, ought men to love their wives as their own bodies. He that loveth his wife loveth himself. For no man ever yet hated his own flesh; but nourished and cherished it, even as the Lord the church: For we are members of his body, of his flesh, and of his bones. For this cause shall a man leave his father and mother, and shall be joined unto his wife, and they shall two shall be one flesh. This is a great mystery; but I speak concerning Christ and the church. Nevertheless, let every one of you in particular so love his wife even as himself; and the wife sees that she reverences her husband"* ***(Ephesians 5:22-33)***.

- ❖ *"Likewise, ye wives, be in subjection to your own husbands; that, if any obey not the Word, they also may without the Word be won by the conversation of the wives"* **(I Peter 3:1)**.

- ❖ *"Likewise, ye husbands, dwell with them according to knowledge, giving honor unto the wife, as unto the weaker vessel, and as being heirs together of the grace of life; that your prayers be not hindered"* **(I Peter 3:7)**.

As we embark on the journey of marriage, we are guided by these profound truths, shaping the love we share. In yielding to one another, we honor the sanctity of our union and create a life filled with love, togetherness, and harmonious unity.

Marriage Testimonial: A Love Anchored in Faith

Our marriage stands as a testament to success, deeply rooted in the intimate communion we share with our Heavenly Father, God. In the essence of His LOVE, we find our strength, echoing the profound truth that we LOVE because He first LOVED us (*1 John 4:19*).

Guided by the timeless wisdom of *1 Corinthians 13:8*, our union thrives in the fertile ground of patience, kindness, meekness, and temperance. Even when we stray towards the extremes, the Lord, in His gentle wisdom, steers us back to the center, where He reigns as the core of our individual beings, allowing us to remain wholly ourselves and truly become one flesh.

Our marriage is a living testament to the three-strand cord—the divine intertwining of God, my husband, and me. As men are visually oriented and thrive on respect, I endeavor to maintain a physical presence that pleases my husband. Recognizing my body as His and submitting to Him in all things becomes an act of love, an offering unto the Lord.
In return, I, as his wife, seek the security and affection that mirror Christ's profound love for the Church, a sacrificial love that gave life.

In essence, we strive to let our lives mirror our Divine Covenant, understanding that our marriage serves a purpose greater than ourselves. Balancing expectations, avoiding the extremes of overestimation and undermining, fosters the of a joyous and fulfilling marriage. We are two servants, devoted to serving each other. Gratitude fills our hearts for the exemplary influence of Mr. & Mrs. Pollard, the wisdom found in their inspiring book, and the guidance from Cross My Heart Ministries. May every marriage touched by these words be blessed with enduring longevity and the eternal rewards that marriage graciously offers. As a constant reminder, "Love never fails" (*1 Corinthians 13:8*).

With heartfelt warmth,

The Ewings,

Celebrating 11 years of a blissful marriage.

Marriage Quotes: Gems of Wisdom

> *"Every love story is beautiful, but ours is my favorite" (Ennvee).*
>
> *"A good marriage is not just about marrying the right person; it is also about being the right person" (Marriage Bible Quotes on Pinterest).*
>
> *"A perfect Marriage is just two imperfect people who refuse to give up On Each Other" (Marriage Quotes Image).*

"A successful marriage requires falling in love many times, always with the same person" (Christian Marriage Quote).

"True love stands by each other's side on good days and stands even closer on bad days" (Inspirational Love & Marriage).

"Happiness in marriage is a moment-by-moment choice. A decision to love, forgive, grow and grow older together" (Fawn Weaver).

"Marriage is a gift from God to us. The quality of our marriage is a gift from us to Him" (L. Whitney Clayton).

"Marriage the Lifelong Journey of Learning to Love Like Christ" (Fiercemarriage.com).

Journal

Chapter Seven
FINDING HAPPINESS WITHIN

Lord, I humbly entreat you, may the love bestowed upon us be an enduring flame, flickering with the eternal warmth of your divine grace. Let our words be a source of kindness, uplifting and constructing rather than tearing down. Always guide us to acknowledge you first, drawing wisdom from your boundless examples. May empathy and consideration for each other's feelings become the cornerstone of our union, and may we continually be attuned to each other's needs and desires.

Father, grant us the strength to be more understanding and forgiving in moments of human weakness. Fortify our faith, instilling a trust that transcends worldly uncertainties. May your wisdom illuminate our lives and guide our expressions of love. Bless our marriage with a peace that surpasses understanding, and may our love be a beacon of your glory, resonating both in the present and for eternity. In Jesus' name, I offer this heartfelt prayer. Amen!

Reflecting on my marital journey, each experience has woven the tapestry of a credible witness on marriage. Through highs and lows, I've grown more appreciative of the profound blessing of being married to a man who wholeheartedly loves me. Marriage has been my guide, teaching me to find my happy place and maintain harmony in my space.

Being a credible witness involves providing reliable evidence, and my marriage, through its trials and triumphs, stands as a testament to enduring love. Reminded of a childhood melody that echoes emotions and inner messages, I see how God has made my marriage credible, a testimony to His faithfulness. I urge you to prioritize God in your union; let Him be the cornerstone of your journey and witness your marriage flourish with lasting goodness. My heartfelt desire is for your happiness, anchored in a steadfast belief in your commitment. I've shared five proven steps that have enriched my journey, and I encourage you to embrace them. God desires to bless your marriage; let His Word shield and uplift you. Date each other, invest quality time, and shift focus from losses to the excitement of what lies ahead. Faith without action is empty, so actively work on your marriage.

Maintain an open mind, recalling the initial attraction that sparked your connection. As the saying goes, "Success means nothing if you don't know the meaning of sacrifice" (Unknown). I share my successes to inspire you to make your marriage a credible witness to the divine union. Rekindle your love; embrace a spirit of expectancy. Believe in God's goodness and let your marriage be a gift for others to witness.

Remember, life grants us one opportunity. Be a voice for marriage, an advocate with the power to instill confidence and self-esteem in others. You might be the catalyst someone needs for informed decisions. Makes a difference that resonates, seek God first, and witness everything falling into divine alignment.

In the immortal words of *Jeremiah 31:3, "The Lord hath appeared of old unto me, saying, Yea, I have loved thee with an everlasting love: therefore, with lovingkindness have I drawn thee."* Life is a singular chance, and you hold advocacy status for marriage. Choose to be the voice that brings hope and makes a difference that transcends time. *"Relationships last long not because they're destined to last long. Relationships last because two brave people made a choice – to keep it, fight for it, and work for it" (Spiritual Quote).*

Journal

Chapter Eight
A JOURNEY OF NEW BEGINNINGS

In "Credible Witness Credible Marriage", there are "Five Proven Steps For a Successful Marriage," my primary audience is couples, and my motivation stems from the enduring nature of my own marriage and witnessing the heartache of friends who've faced divorce. I wholeheartedly reject the idea that a union blessed by God should ever be shattered. A successful marriage, in my eyes, involves honor, accountability, persistence, patience, and a mutual willingness to yield to each other.

Prioritizing one another and fostering each other's growth is of paramount importance. It all comes down to being intentional in your love and commitment.

Proverbs 18:22 wisely tells us, "Whoso findeth a wife findeth a good thing and obtaineth favor of the Lord." Often, this verse is misconstrued. It doesn't say, "she who findeth a husband." I firmly believe that the foundation of a thriving marriage rests on embracing biblical values. With 38 years of marriage, I've gathered a wealth of experience.

To unshackle your marriage from any limitations, you must be willing to continually reignite the flames of passion. It all begins with happiness, but it's a deeper happiness than you might think. Don't allow your current circumstances to dictate your emotions. Strive to elevate your relationship to new heights of happiness. Remember that marriage is a gift you offer to the world; let its radiance shine brightly. Be assured that God's love for you knows no bounds.

We are given one precious opportunity to live life and discover inner peace. Envision the profound impact of such a life. Some couples may find themselves navigating marital crises, and they might need your guidance to make a difference. Remember that the Lord answers prayers according to His divine will, and He wishes for us to witness His grace within our marriages. Is your marriage a Kingdom marriage, one that inspires and uplifts other unions? Rediscover the joy that initially brought you together and share it generously.

With God by your side, every day can be one filled with victory and joy, His guidance ordering your steps even in times of crisis. In the wise words of an unknown source, "Relationships last not merely because they're destined to, but because two courageous individuals make a choice—to preserve it, to fight for it, and to work for it" (Spiritual Quote).

Embarking on the journey of new beginnings is a perpetual exploration, a constant surrender to the divine guidance of God. We willingly allow Him to lead, guide, and direct us along a path that we perceive as not just a personal journey but a beacon of hope and assistance for fellow couples, whether young or seasoned. It's a path etched with the wisdom gained from facing challenges and learning to navigate the inevitable pitfalls that accompany the journey toward a resilient and thriving marriage.

The essence lies in the profound truth that, for new beginnings to unfold, one must undergo experiences that mark an ending. These transitions become the tapestry of growth, a canvas on which the colors of resilience, love, and shared wisdom are painted. In embracing these endings, we discover the strength to forge ahead, armed with the lessons that pave the way for hopeful beginnings.

May our journey not only serve as a testament to personal growth but also as a guidepost for others traversing similar paths. With God as our navigator, we aim to illuminate the way for those grappling with the complexities of marital dynamics, offering solace and inspiration to overcome the challenges that may arise. In the fabric of life, each ending woven into our story becomes a thread in the fabric of new beginnings, an unfolding narrative that we graciously share with others. As we navigate the twists and turns, we find purpose in turning our experiences into a compass, directing those in need toward the hopeful promise of new beginnings.

Journal

ABOUT THE AUTHOR

Meet Anetria Pollard, a seasoned relationship coach celebrated for her expertise in sustaining love through the decades. Married for an impressive 38 years to Roderick Pollard Sr., Anetria draws from personal experience, infusing her guidance with a deep understanding of the journey of lifelong love.

She is also the award-winning author of "Cross My Heart From Hurt To Healing," a book that has garnered acclaim for its transformative insights. With a steadfast commitment to "Rekindling Lifelong Partnerships," Anetria shares her wisdom, offering readers a roadmap to enduring, fulfilling relationships.

Contact Information

Website: www.anetriapollard.com

Email: info@anetriapollard.com

Facebook: @anetria.spearspollard

Instagram: @anetriapollard

LinkedIn: https://www.linkedin.com/in/anetria-pollard-8a524b112/

JOURNAL

ANETRIA POLLARD
anetriapollard.com

Made in the USA
Coppell, TX
29 February 2024

29594353R00056